VOLCANOES

A TRUE BOOK

by

Paul P. Sipiera

Children's Press®
A Division of Grolier Publishing

New York London Hong Kong Sydney
Danbury, Connecticut

Reading Consultant
Linda Cornwell
Learning Resource Consultant
Indiana Department
of Education

Author's Dedication
To Tony Reay, together we
studied the old volcanoes at
Kakanui, New Zealand

An erupting volcano

Visit Children's Press on the Internet at:
http://publishing.grolier.com

Library of Congress Cataloging-in-Publication Data

Sipiera, Paul P.
   Volcanoes / by Paul P. Sipiera.
     p. cm. — (A true book)
   Includes bibliographical references and index.
   Summary: Introduces the origins, causes, and destructive effects of
volcanoes.
   ISBN: 0-516-20681-8 (lib.bdg.)   0-516-26444-3 (pbk.)
   1. Volcanoes—Juvenile literature. [1. Volcanoes.] I. Title.
II. Series.
QE521.3.S573 1998
551.21—dc21   97-34931
                                                               CIP
                                                                AC

Contents

This volcano is located at Hawaii Volcanoes National Park in Hawaii.

Where Do Volcanoes Begin?

A volcano is a mountain with an opening called a crater. When a volcano erupts, hot gases, ash, rocks, and lava can be thrown out of its crater. Volcanoes form because the inside of Earth is very hot. When a volcano erupts, some of this heat escapes into the air.

Earth

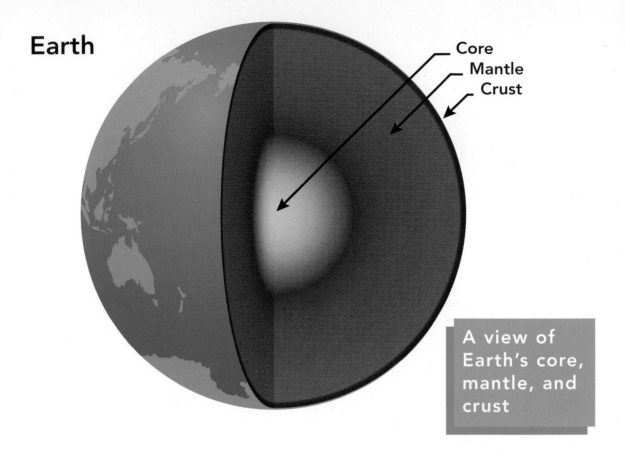

Core
Mantle
Crust

A view of Earth's core, mantle, and crust

Scientists divide Earth into three parts: the core, the mantle, and the crust. The core lies deep below Earth's surface. It has two parts. One part is liquid, or melted, metal. The other part is made up of solid metal.

Just above the core lies Earth's mantle. In the mantle, temperatures are hot enough to soften rock. The rock is soft enough to squeeze—like toothpaste inside a tube. This soft rock is called magma. Sometimes magma flows into cracks near Earth's surface. When magma flows out of Earth through a volcano, it is

Lava flows can look like rivers of fire.

called lava. When the lava cools, it hardens to form rock.

The crust forms Earth's surface. It is divided into huge pieces called plates. There are about ten large plates and about twenty smaller ones.

Sometimes plates bump into each other. As a result, one plate is pushed down deeper inside Earth. When this happens, magma may be pushed to the surface. This can cause

Earth's plates move at about the same rate as your fingernails grow.

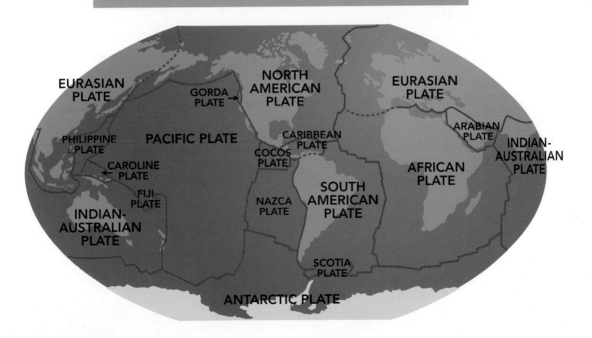

EURASIAN PLATE

GORDA PLATE →

NORTH AMERICAN PLATE

EURASIAN PLATE

ARABIAN PLATE

INDIAN-AUSTRALIAN PLATE

PHILIPPINE PLATE

PACIFIC PLATE

CARIBBEAN PLATE

COCOS PLATE

AFRICAN PLATE

← CAROLINE PLATE

FIJI PLATE

NAZCA PLATE

SOUTH AMERICAN PLATE

INDIAN-AUSTRALIAN PLATE

SCOTIA PLATE

ANTARCTIC PLATE

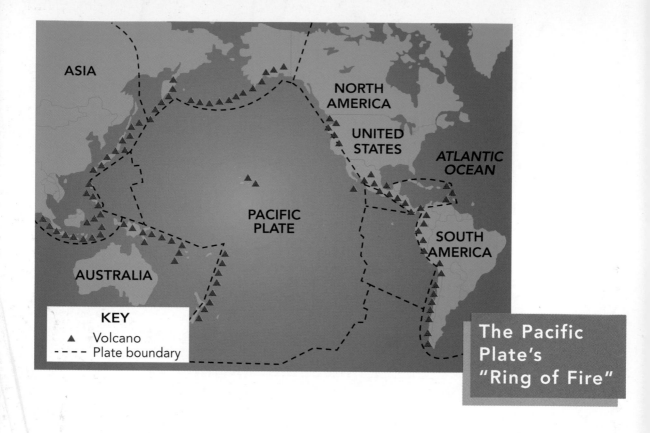

ASIA

NORTH AMERICA

UNITED STATES

ATLANTIC OCEAN

PACIFIC PLATE

SOUTH AMERICA

AUSTRALIA

KEY
▲ Volcano
- - - Plate boundary

The Pacific Plate's "Ring of Fire"

a volcanic eruption. There are many volcanoes along the edge of the Pacific Plate. There are so many volcanoes in this area that it is called the "Ring of Fire."

Out of This World Volcanoes

A 1996 photograph of Io

There is one place that has more active volcanoes than Earth. It is Io, one of the four largest moons of Jupiter. On Io, volcanic eruptions are so common that the moon's surface gets completely covered with lava every 1,000 years.

In this photograph, the dark spots are Io's volcanoes.

Different Kinds of Volcanoes

Volcanoes come in three different shapes. The names used to describe them are: shield (SHEELD), composite (kuhm-POZ-it), or cinder (SIN-dur) cone.

A shield volcano is wider than it is high. A composite

Types of Volcanoes

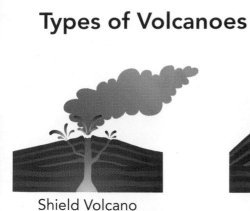

Shield Volcano

Cinder Cone

Composite Volcano

The three kinds of volcanoes are: shield (left), cinder cone (center), and composite (right).

volcano looks like a tall mountain with steep sides. A cinder cone is a cone-shaped hill. It is much smaller than a shield or a composite volcano. It is usually less than 1,000 feet

Hawaii's Mauna Loa (above) is a shield volcano. California's Mount Shasta (right) is a composite volcano.

(1,600 meters) high. But it has very steep sides.

These three types of volcanoes have different kinds of eruptions. The eruptions of shield volcanoes are quiet. But

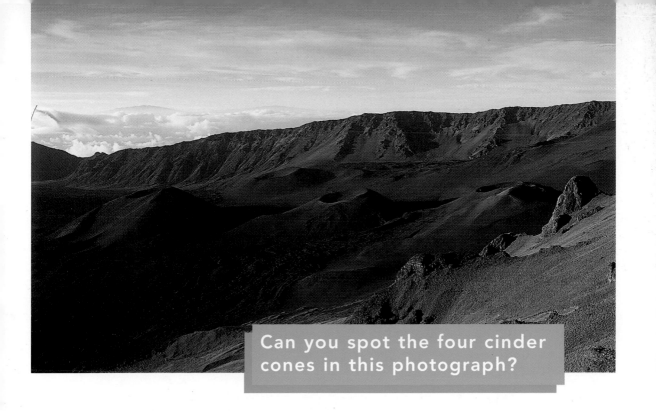

Can you spot the four cinder cones in this photograph?

there can be a lot of lava that flows out of it. Composite volcanoes can have either great explosions or quiet lava flows. Some cinder cones form after a composite volcano has a great explosion.

What Makes a Volcano Erupt?

No two volcanic eruptions are exactly the same. Before every volcanic eruption, there is a series of small earthquakes. These earthquakes occur because magma from deep inside Earth presses against the rocks just below Earth's surface. When the force of the magma is very strong, the rocks break. This causes the small earthquakes. After the rocks break, the magma moves closer to Earth's surface. If this continues, the magma will eventually break through the surface and build up to form a volcano.

Besides soft rock, magma also contains water. If there is a lot of water in the magma, the eruption will be violent.

A tower of steam rises from Mount Pinatubo in the Philippines.

You can see this water during a volcanic eruption. It is in the "smoke" that rises from the volcano. The smoke is really a mixture of steam (water that has turned into a gas) and ash.

Volcanic Features

The eruption of a volcano can produce many interesting features, especially in its lava flows. One type of lava flow is called pahoehoe (pah-HOY-hoy). This lava forms smooth rock when it cools. Another lava flow is called aa (AH-ah). Aa has a rough, jagged

Some lava flows make a smooth rock called pahoehoe (top). Other flows make jagged rocks called aa (center). Some lava trees have existed for hundreds of years (right).

shape. When lava flows into the ocean, its quickly cools into a shape known as pillow lava. Lava flows can also create "lava trees" as they pass through a forest. This happens when the hot lava surrounds the trunk of a tree. The upper part of the tree burns away. The lower part of the tree hardens into rock as the lava cools.

Volcanic activity has created some unique places on Earth. When magma is just below

Earth's surface, it heats the groundwater above it. Sometimes, the groundwater gets so hot that it explodes out of the ground. This is called a geyser. One of the world's most famous geysers is called Old Faithful. It is located at Yellowstone National Park in Wyoming.

Many interesting volcanic features occur underground. Often, they can only be seen after erosion uncovers them.

Old Faithful geyser got its name because it follows a schedule of eruption—about once every seventy-seven minutes.

(Erosion is the slow wearing away of Earth's surface by wind or water.) In the United

States, Devil's Tower, in Wyoming, and Ship Rock, in New Mexico, are really the necks of old volcanoes.

Devil's Tower (left) and Ship Rock (below)

Inside South Africa's diamond pipes, miners drill in search of valuable diamonds.

Another interesting volcanic feature is the diamond pipes of South Africa. Some of the most valuable diamonds in the world have been found inside these volcanic pipes.

Famous Volcanic Eruptions

You may have heard about the modern-day volcanic eruptions on Hawaii. But these eruptions seem small compared to others that have occurred in the past. A gigantic volcanic eruption created the Yellowstone Basin in Wyoming. Another

This is one of many recent eruptions of Hawaii's Kilauea volcano.

Nearly 2,000 feet (610 meters) deep, Crater Lake is the deepest lake in the United States. (The small island inside the lake, Wizard Island, is a cinder cone.)

great eruption resulted in the formation of Crater Lake in Oregon.

One of the most famous volcanic eruptions took place

in Italy in the year A.D. 79. Mount Vesuvius erupted, and the city of Pompeii was destroyed.

Mount Vesuvius is a composite volcano. When it erupted, it exploded with great force.

A present-day photograph of Italy's Mount Vesuvius

These columns (top) are all that remain of an ancient home destroyed when Mount Vesuvius erupted in A.D. 79. Throughout Pompeii, the shapes of victims' bodies were preserved by the ash and cinder from the eruption (bottom). Today, many of the bodies remain where they were found.

Cinder and ash buried the city. For almost 2,000 years, Pompeii was buried and nearly forgotten. It was uncovered in 1748 by archeologists. (Archeologists are scientists who study the past by digging up buildings and objects.) The archeologists found that the ash and cinder that buried the city had protected it. The city looked almost the same as it did on the day of the eruption. Today, scientists continue to uncover and to study Pompeii.

Krakatoa

The noise from Krakatoa's explosion is believed to be the loudest sound in Earth's history.

One of the largest volcanic eruptions ever recorded on Earth occurred on August 27, 1883. An island volcano called Krakatoa, in Indonesia, exploded. The sound was heard 3,000 miles (4,800 kilometers) away. The eruption caused huge waves that were 120 feet (37 meters) high. A cloud of dust rose 50 miles (80 km) into the atmosphere, and 36,000 people were killed.

In 1902, Mount Pelee, on the island of Martinique, erupted. The city of St. Pierre was completely destroyed. A fiery cloud raced down the

The town of St. Pierre, Martinique, lies in ruins following the 1902 eruption of Mount Pelee.

mountain at 125 miles (200 km) per hour. In less than five minutes, almost 28,000 people were killed.

The 1980 eruption of Mount St. Helens was similar to the eruption of Mount Pelee. Mount St. Helens is located in Washington State. Its eruption blew off a huge section of the volcano. A fiery cloud was released. It caused terrible destruction. Many of the people living in the area

Mount St. Helens and the surrounding area were covered by ash for months after the volcano erupted on May 18, 1980.

left before the eruption. However, fifty-seven people who lived near the volcano were killed.

Effects of Volcanoes

Volcanoes such as Mount St. Helens and Mount Fuji (Japan) surround the Pacific Ocean. Other dangerous volcanoes exist along the western coasts of North America, South America, and Mexico. Living near a volcano means living with the threat of an eruption.

People who live in cities located near volcanoes live with the danger of a volcanic eruption. (This is Shizuoka City, near Mount Fuji, Japan.)

If an eruption occurs, there is the chance for great loss of life and property.

Volcanic eruptions also have an effect on the world's weather and climate. Weather

After Mount Pinatubo, in the Philippines, erupted, ash "rained" on cars, streets, and homes for days.

is the condition of the outside air at a certain time, or in a certain place. Climate is the kind of weather that a place has over a long period of time. When a volcano erupts, it sends huge amounts of ash, dust, and dangerous gases into the air. Ash clouds from a volcanic eruption can climb to more than 7 miles (12 km) high. Parts of these clouds can

Ash clouds can rise several miles into the sky.

Ash from a volcanic eruption can make daytime dark. Streetlights go on and vehicle headlights are needed because the ash blocks out the sun.

remain in the air for more than two years. These clouds can block out sunlight. This results in a shorter season in which to grow food. This happened in 1815, after the eruption of Mount Tambora in Indonesia.

As the ash from the eruption of Mount Tambora spread through the atmosphere, it affected the world's weather. The spring and summer of 1816 were especially cold. People called it the "year without summer." There were even heavy

A massive volcanic eruption can result in the destruction of crops by disrupting the weather.

snows in the northeastern part of North America in June, July, and August! This destroyed many crops. Some people faced starvation.

The eruption of a volcano can disrupt the weather all over the world. The ash that fell from Mount St. Helens created a cool, damp, and cloudy summer for eastern Canada in 1980. This can happen when only one volcano erupts. Imagine what could happen if several large volcanoes erupted at the same time. It would certainly affect the world's climate, and would change life as we know it.

This is a 1997 photograph of the island of Montserrat, located in the Caribbean Sea. Montserrat has been almost completely destroyed by volcanic eruptions.

To Find Out More

Here are some additional resources to help you learn more about volcanoes:

 **Books**

Arnold, Nick. **Volcano, Earthquake, and Hurricane.** Raintree Steck-Vaughn, 1997.

Krafft, Maurice. **Volcano!** Forest House, 1993.

Lye, Keith. **Volcanoes.** Raintree Steck-Vaughn, 1996.

Murray, Peter. **Volcanos.** Child's World, 1995.

Nelson, Sharlene and Ted. **Mount St. Helens National Volcanic Monument.** Children's Press, 1997.

Walker, Jane. **Volcanoes.** Millbrook Press, 1995.

Walker, Sally. **Volcanoes: Earth's Inner Fire.** Lerner, 1994.

💡 Organizations and Online Sites

Earth's Active Volcanoes

http://www.geo.mtu.edu/ volcanoes/world.html

Giant world map with active volcanoes numbered for quick reference and corresponding links to each site, including photos and information.

United States Geological Survey

804 National Center
Reston, VA 20192
http://www.usgs.gov

Mount St. Helens

http://www.teleport.com/ ~longview/msh.html

Learn more about the 1980 eruption of this volcano, the devastation it caused to animals, vegetation, and property, and the regrowth that has followed. This site has great photos!

Volcanoes

http://www.volcanoes.com

This site is an index of other sites related to volcanoes, as well as a registry of volcano links from around the world.

Volcano World

http://volcano.und.nodak. edu/

This site is full of interesting information. You can see a map of currently erupting volcanoes, visit volcanic parks and monuments, see video clips of volcanic eruptions, enter a drawing contest, play games, and much more!

Important Words

ash dust-sized rock material that is blown out of a volcano

atmosphere gases that surround a planet

feature important part or quality of something

groundwater water trapped within rock, sand, or gravel beneath Earth's surface

lava hot liquid that flows from a volcano, turns to rock when it cools

unique uncommon, special

Index

Meet the Author

Paul P. Sipiera is a professor of geology and astronomy at William Rainey Harper College in Palatine, Illinois. His main research interests are in the study of meteorites, volcanoes, and Antarctica. Paul lives with his wife Diane and their three daughters, Andrea, Paula, and Caroline, on their small farm in Galena, Illinois.